OF GODS, GODDESSES, TEMPLES AND PRIESTS

Ancient Egypt History Facts Books Children's Ancient History

BABY PROFESSOR
EDUCATION KIDS

Speedy Publishing LLC

40 E. Main St. #1156

Newark, DE 19711

www.speedypublishing.com

Copyright 2017

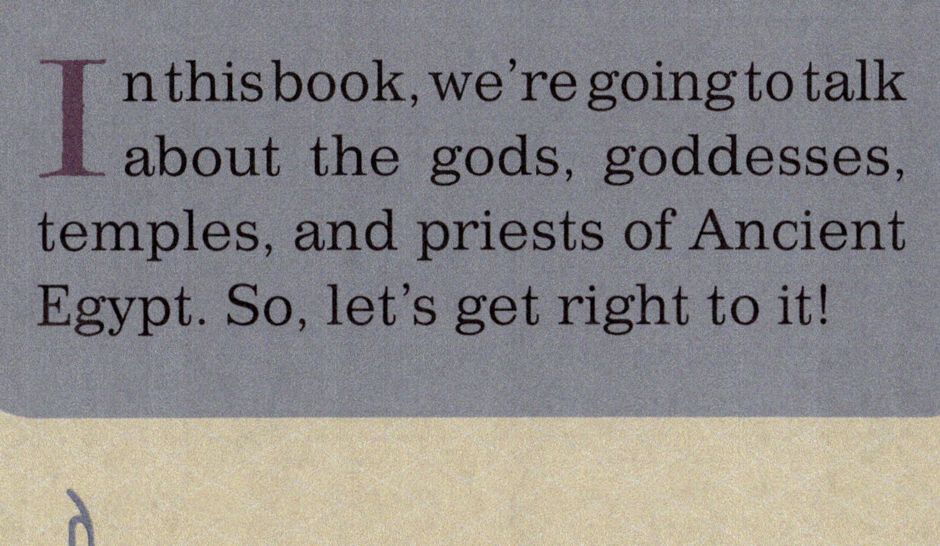

In this book, we're going to talk about the gods, goddesses, temples, and priests of Ancient Egypt. So, let's get right to it!

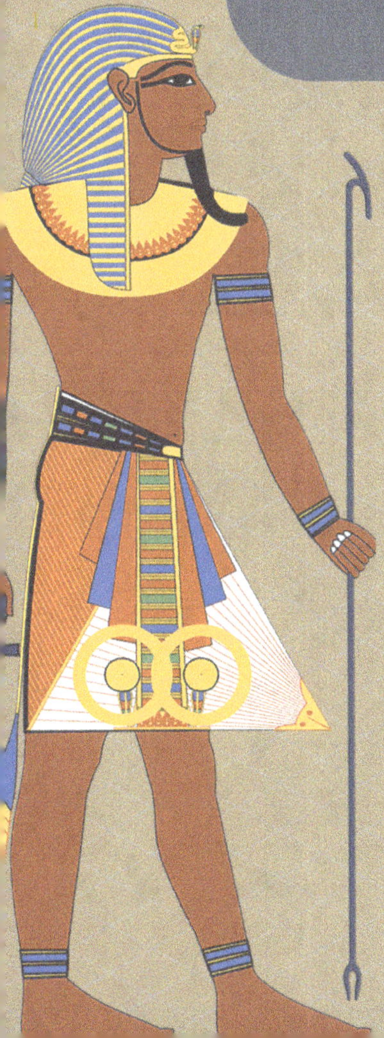

Ancient people didn't fully understand the natural processes happening around them every day. To makes sense of their world, they used religion and mythology to represent both the natural and the supernatural. The Egyptians had hundreds of gods and goddesses in their religion. Each god or goddess had a specific role to play. Some were more important than others.

THE FORMS AND CHARACTERS OF GODS AND GODDESSES

Many of the Egyptian gods and goddesses represented an important physical part of the world. For example, Nut was the sky goddess and Ra was the sun god. However, their characters weren't always consistent. Sometimes they were kind and good to people, but at other times they were angry and vengeful. Some of the gods were constantly changing their personalities.

The gods and goddesses generally showed up with the heads of animals and the bodies of humans. However, depending on their moods, this could change as well. For example, if a goddess was angry she could be shown with the head of a roaring lion and the body of a person. If she was in a peaceful mood, she might be shown with a cat's head and a woman's body.

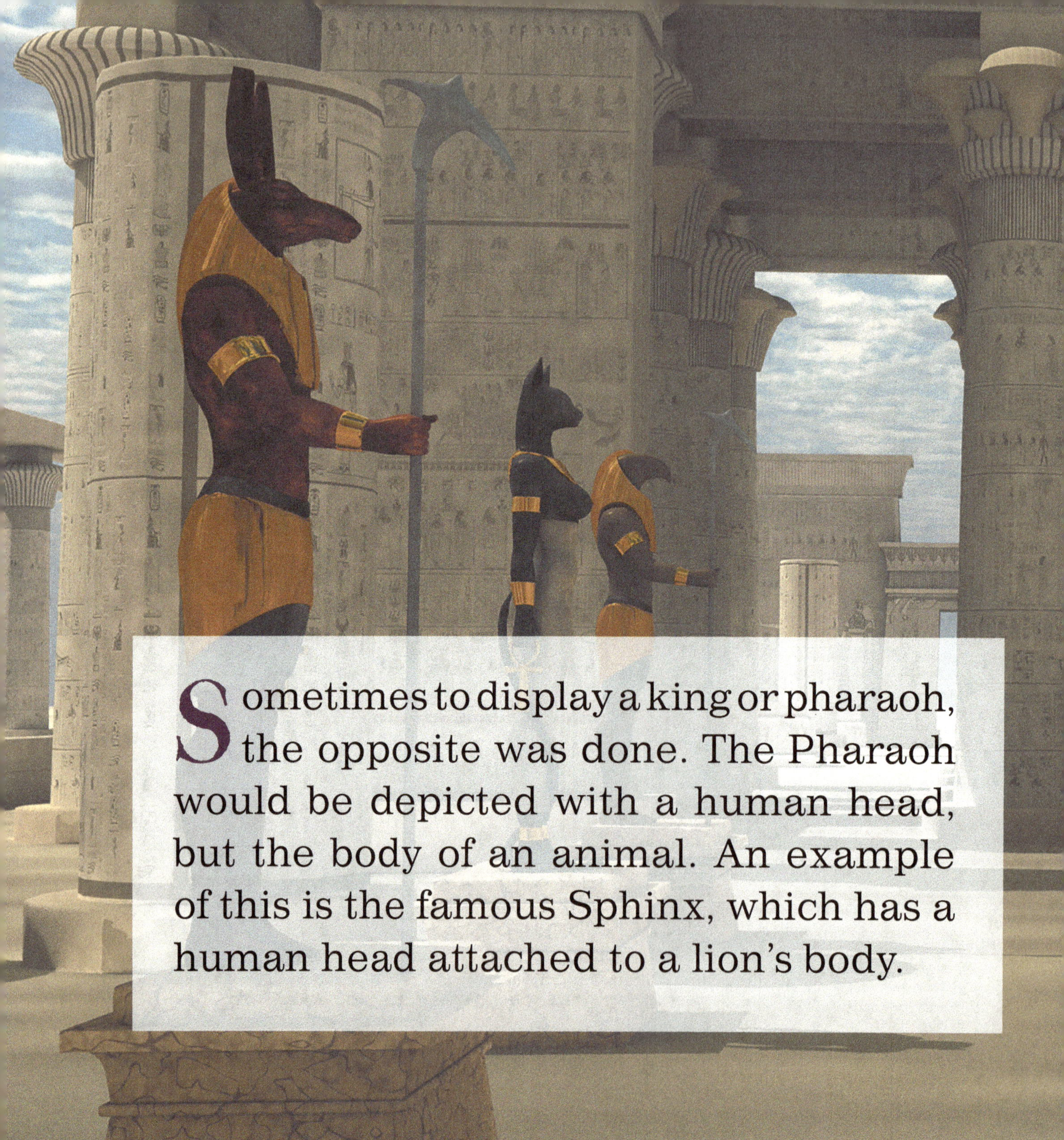

Sometimes to display a king or pharaoh, the opposite was done. The Pharaoh would be depicted with a human head, but the body of an animal. An example of this is the famous Sphinx, which has a human head attached to a lion's body.

Shu and Geb

M any of the gods and goddesses looked just like human beings or exaggerated forms of human beings. The god of the air called Shu and the god of the earth called Geb are two examples of these human-looking gods. There were also a few less important gods that took very strange shapes. The god Bes had a face like a mask. The goddess Taurt had a form that was a combination of a hippo blended with a crocodile.

# THE GOD RA

As in many other primitive religions, the sun god was the most important god. This was true in the Ancient Egyptian religion as well. Their sun god was called Ra and he was depicted with a hawk's head. He wore a headdress that was a disk in the form of the sun.

RA

Isis

THE GODDESS ISIS

Isis was the first daughter of the god of the earth, Geb, and the goddess of the sky, who was called Nut. It was thought that she gave birth to both heaven and earth. She was a popular goddess because she was motherly and a protector to all those who were in need. She wore a headdress depicting a throne.

THE GOD OSIRIS

Osiris was the first mummy. He had originally been a Pharaoh, until his brother Seth killed him and cut his body into pieces. His wife Isis went to find him and she put his body back together with bandages.

Osiris

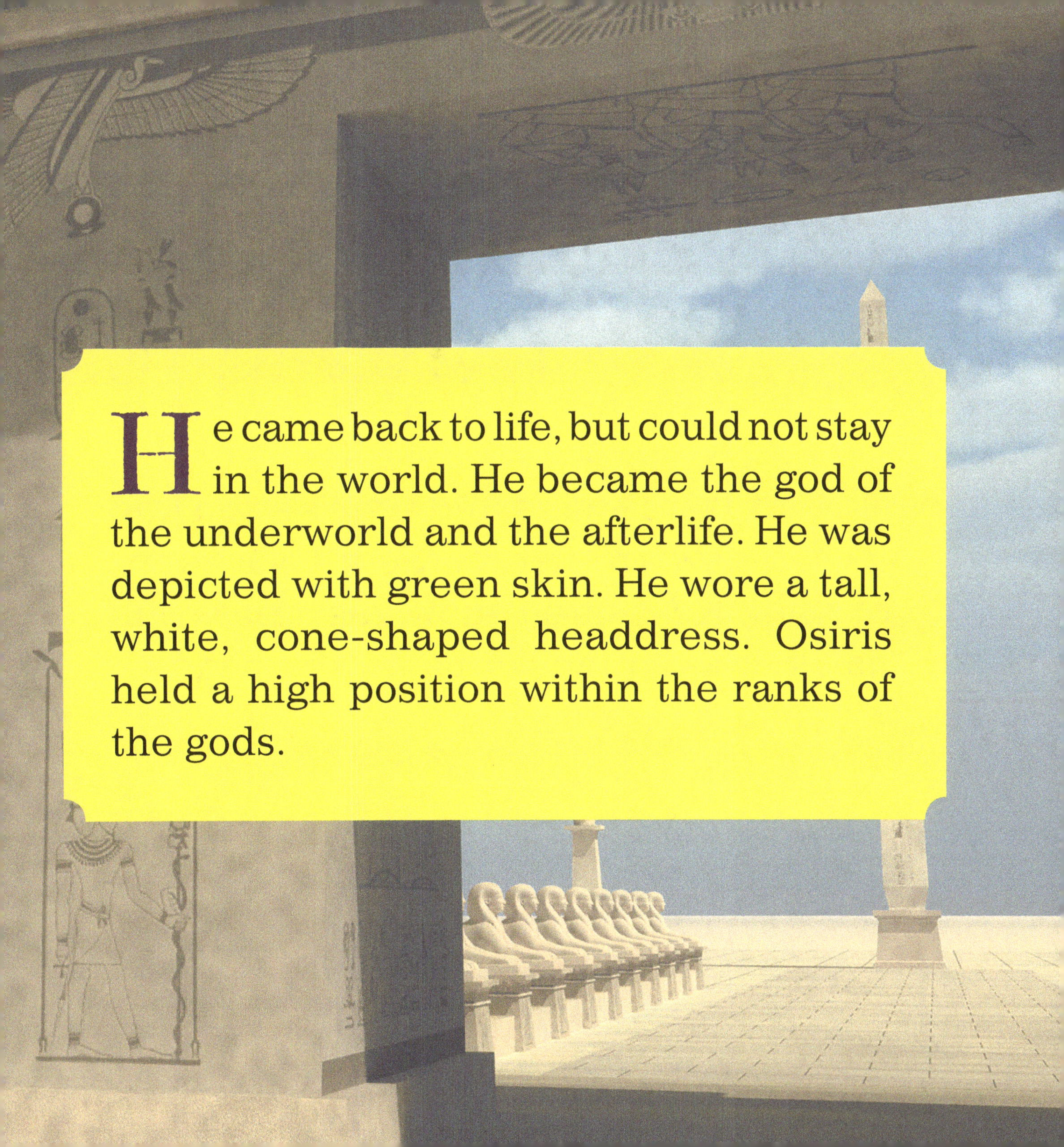

He came back to life, but could not stay in the world. He became the god of the underworld and the afterlife. He was depicted with green skin. He wore a tall, white, cone-shaped headdress. Osiris held a high position within the ranks of the gods.

THE GOD HORUS

Horus was Isis's and Osiris's son and the sworn enemy of Seth, Osiris's evil brother. He is often shown as a powerful hawk or as a man with a hawk's head.

HORUS

HUROS AS FALCON

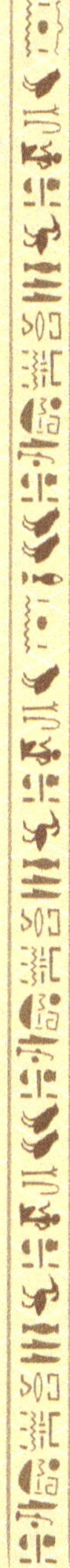

H e ruled the sky and it was thought that he was the protector of the Pharaohs. Over time, it was believed that the Pharaoh was the personification of Horus on Earth, which simply means that the Pharaoh was the divine representative of Horus on Earth.

THE GOD ANUBIS

Anubis was the son of Seth, Osiris's evil brother, and the goddess of mourning and grief, Nephythys. He is depicted with the head of a jackal, which is a skinny wild dog.

Anubis

ANUBIS TENDING A MUMMY

He was important to the process of mummification because he was the protector of those who had passed on to the afterlife. The embalmers who mummified dead people frequently wore masks and headdresses to represent the god Anubis.

THE GOD THOTH

Thoth was the god who inspired all writing as well as all knowledge. He was pictured as having the head of an ibis, which is a type of water bird. He was sometimes pictured as a baboon. He was shown holding a scribe's pen. Thoth was one of the oldest gods and one of his roles was to record a person's deeds at the end of his or her life before the day of judgment.

Thoth

Nut

Nut was the mother of the god Osiris, the goddess Isis, the god Seth, and the goddess Nephythys. She represented the sky and each of her arms and legs represented a direction in the heavens—north, south, east, and west.

Her body was long and stretched out and she was often painted on temple ceilings and the inside of coffins. She swallowed the sun god Ra every night. In the morning, she gave birth to him again. This was the Egyptian way of explaining the disappearance of the sun at night.

Amun

THE GOD AMUN

The city of Thebes was once a tiny town and then it became a very powerful kingdom in the Egyptian civilization. The god Amun, also known as Amen and Ammon, was thought of "as the mysterious one" because he frequently changed form from a ram to a goose and back again.

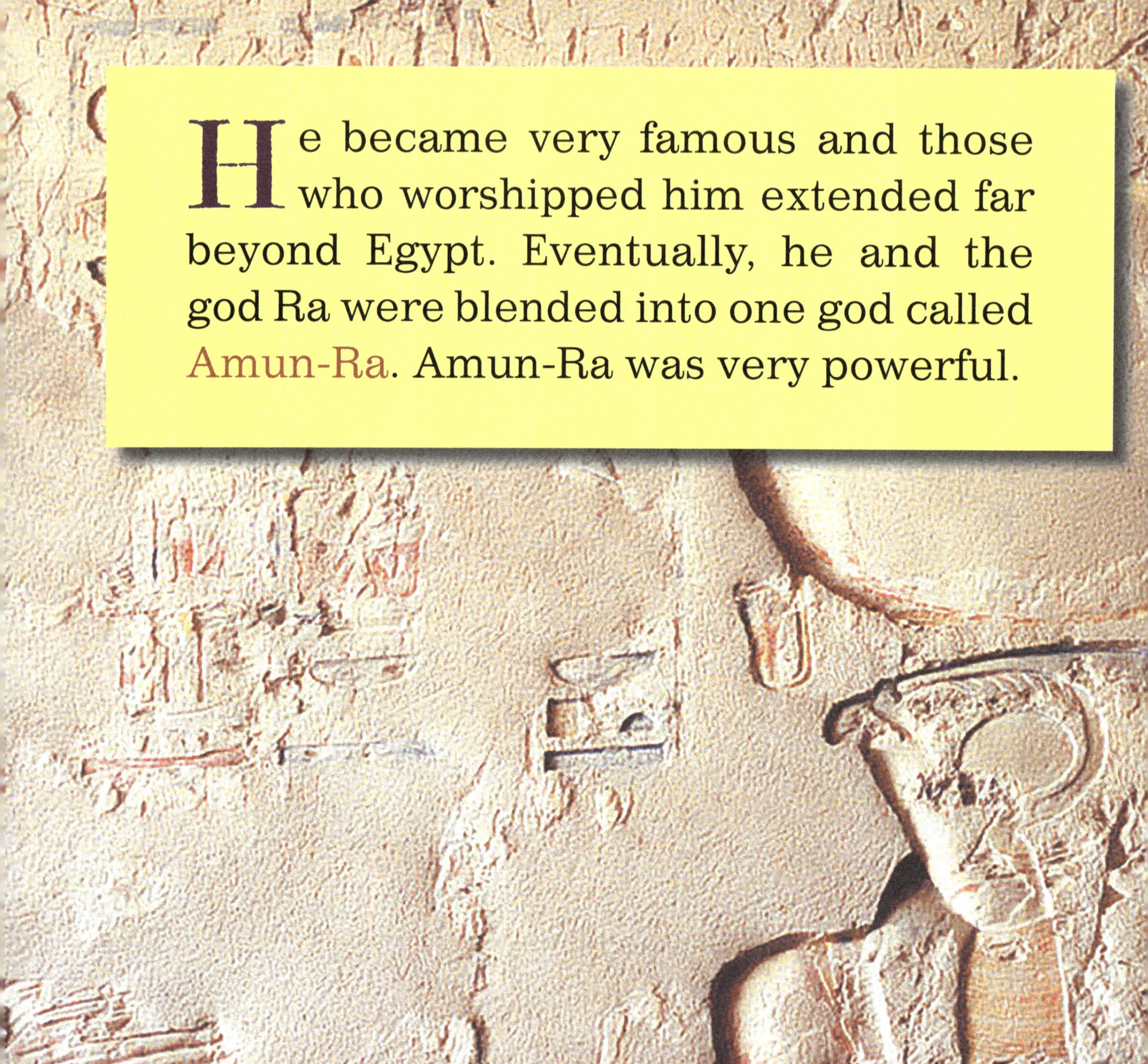

He became very famous and those who worshipped him extended far beyond Egypt. Eventually, he and the god Ra were blended into one god called Amun-Ra. Amun-Ra was very powerful.

Ammit

DEMONS IN THE RELIGION OF ANCIENT EGYPT

In the Egyptian religion, demons were less powerful than gods and goddesses, but they were more powerful than people. They had eternal life and could exist in two places at the same time. They had an influence on both the supernatural and the natural. One of the most important demons was Ammit.

She was a creature who had a body composed of three different animals. She had the head of a crocodile, the front paws of a lion, and the rear end and tail of a hippo. These animals were the fiercest animals that Egyptians encountered. Ammit had a very important role to play in the afterlife.

AMMIT

When a person died, his heart was weighted against a special feather called the "feather of truth and justice." If the person's heart was light as a feather, then it meant that he was good and should

be given entrance into the afterlife. If the person was bad, she had a heavy heart. She would not be given entrance to the afterlife. Instead, that person's heart would be eaten by the scary demon Ammit.

nother important demon in the Egyptian religion was Apepi, who was sometimes called Apophis. This demon was the sun god's enemy. He was shown as a huge snake. He threatened the sun at night and when there was an eclipse of the sun he was blamed for the sun's disappearance.

ADOPHIS

EGYPTIAN MUMMY IN THE SHIP OF RA

THE AFTERLIFE

The Egyptians definitely believed that there was a life after their life on Earth was over. It was important for the body to be recognizable after death because the person would have to unite the two parts of his body together.

The "ka" was the part of the body that had physical life and the "ba" was the spiritual essence or soul of the person. The Egyptians mummified bodies so that the body could be reunited with the soul in the afterlife.

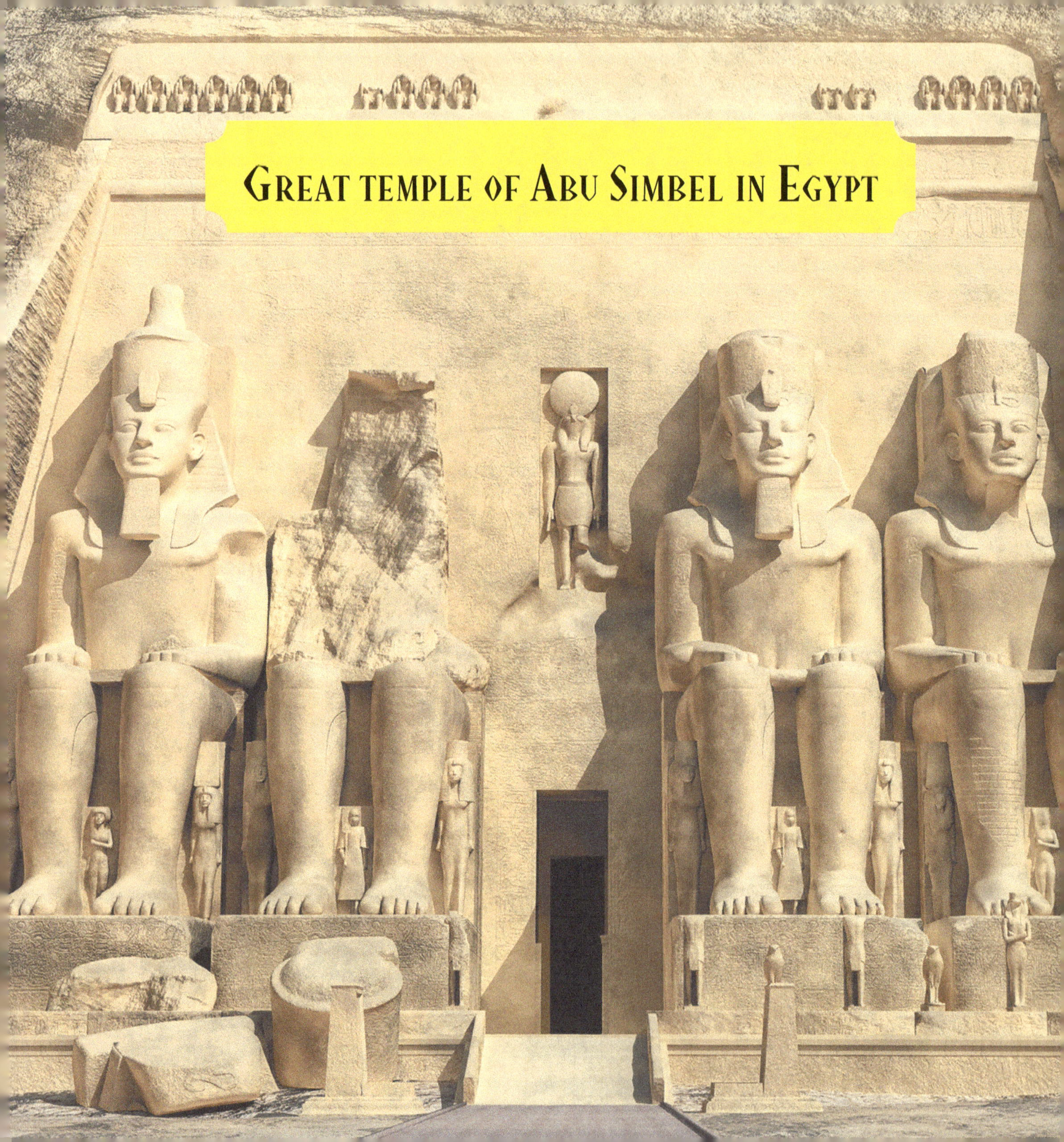
GREAT TEMPLE OF ABU SIMBEL IN EGYPT

The Egyptian rulers were called Pharaohs. They built elaborate temple structures to worship the gods. These temples were primarily a place for worship and were adorned with lush gardens, beautiful statues, and inscribed memorials.

The priests who presided at the temples played a very important role in Egyptian society. The only person who could enter the sacred section of the temple was the priest. The priest could make offerings at the statue that represented the god or goddess that particular temple enshrined. The priest's job was to care for the god or goddess, not the people who worshipped at the temple.

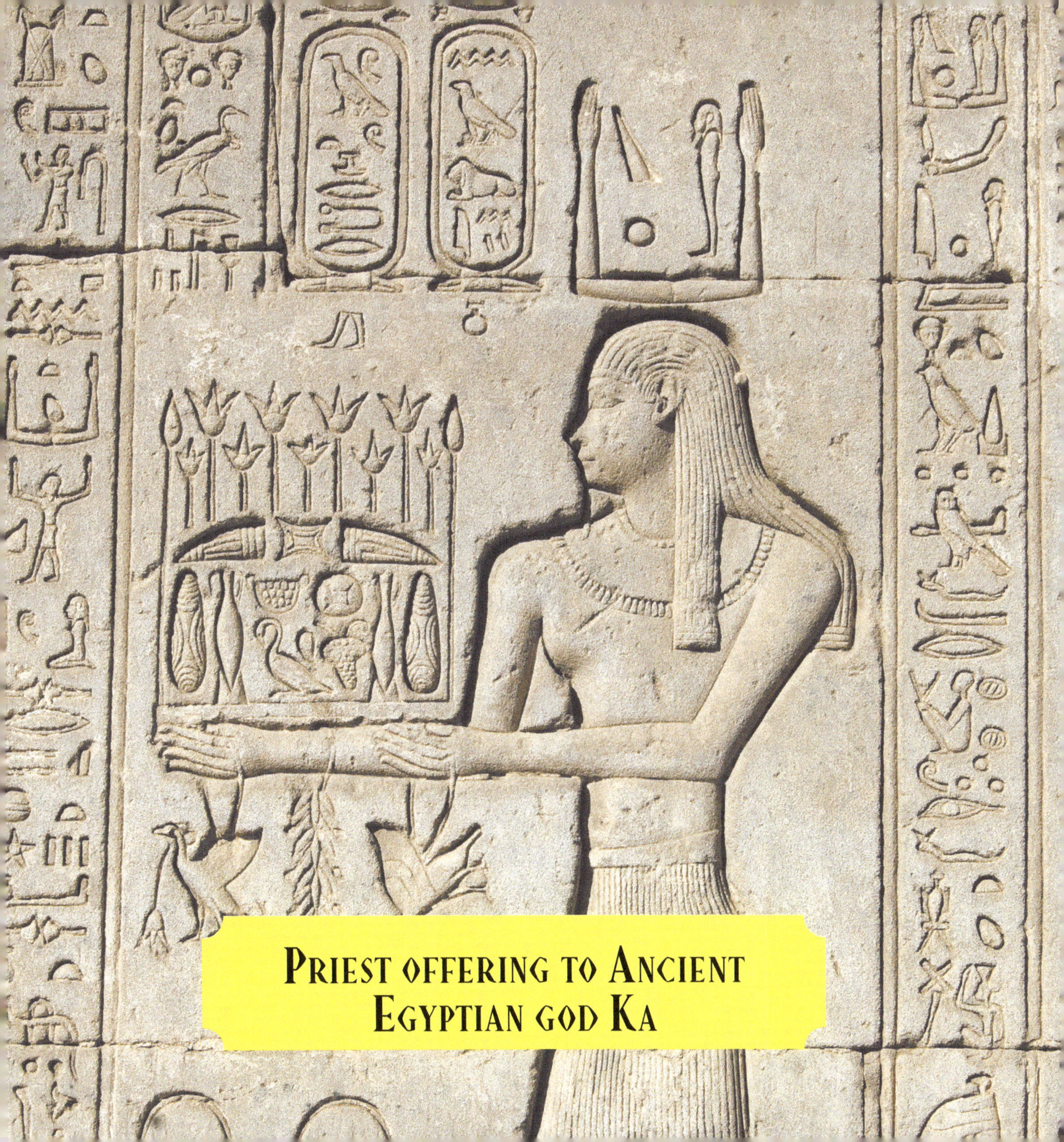

PRIEST OFFERING TO ANCIENT
EGYPTIAN GOD KA

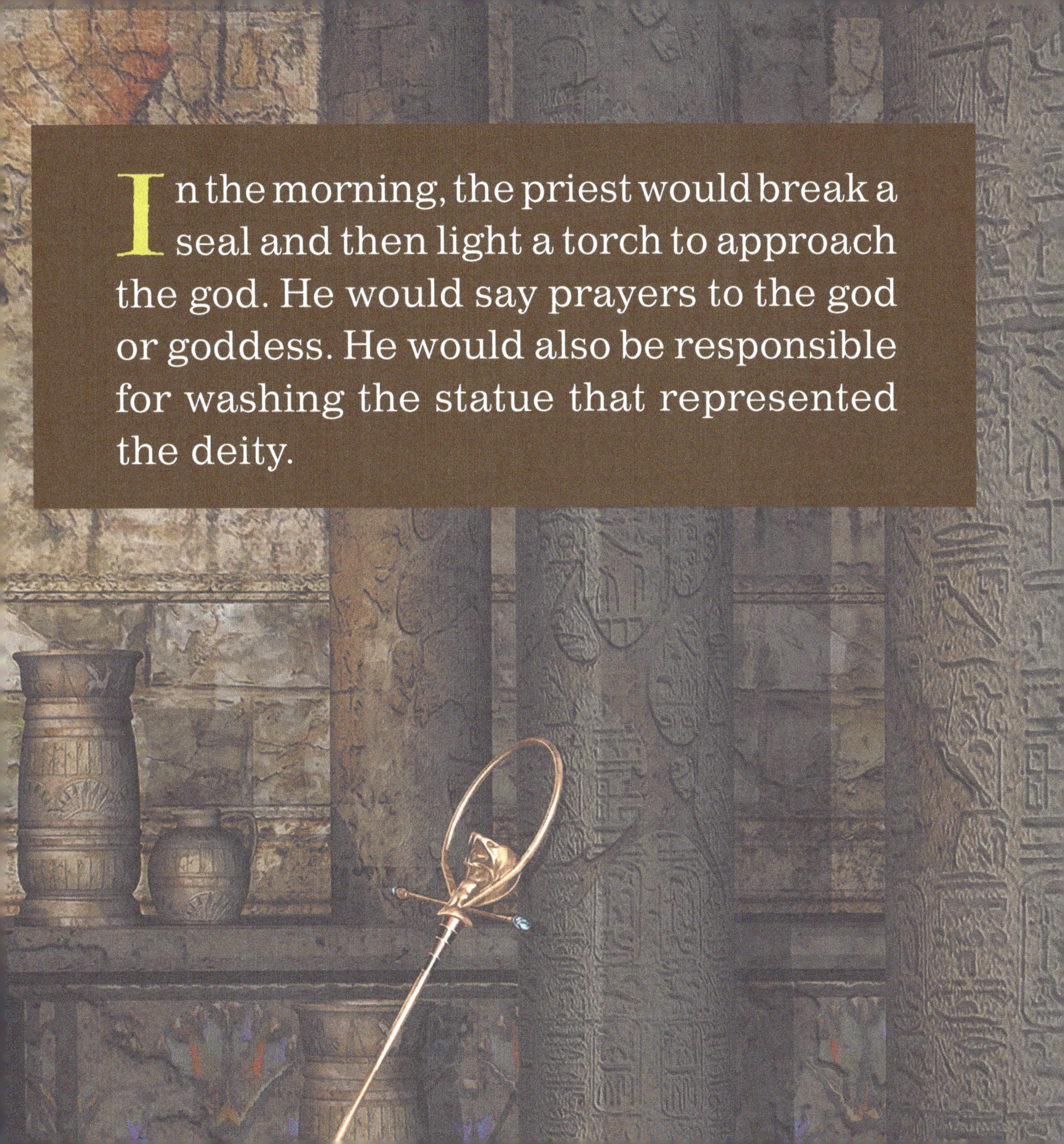

In the morning, the priest would break a seal and then light a torch to approach the god. He would say prayers to the god or goddess. He would also be responsible for washing the statue that represented the deity.

He would place fresh clothing on the statue and adorn it with jewels. At the end of the day, he would sweep away his own footprints before sealing the sacred area for the next day's worship.

The Pharaoh usually selected the new priests. The priests needed to shave their bodies as well as their heads every day. They took cold water baths often throughout the day to purify themselves for their duties in the temple.

Awesome! Now you know more about the gods, goddesses, temples, and priests of Ancient Egypt. You can find more Ancient History books from Baby Professor by searching the website of your favorite book retailer.

Visit
BABY PROFESSOR
EDUCATION KIDS
www.BabyProfessorBooks.com
to download Free Baby Professor eBooks and view
our catalog of new and exciting Children's Books